AWESOME CREATURES OF THE
Atlantic Ocean

Learn About Animals Including the Great White Shark, Sea Turtles, and Dolphins!

Tamra B. Orr

CURIOUS FOX BOOKS

NORTH AMERICA

IRELAND

EUROPE

ATLANTIC OCEAN

AFRICA

SOUTH AMERICA

ATLANTIC OCEAN

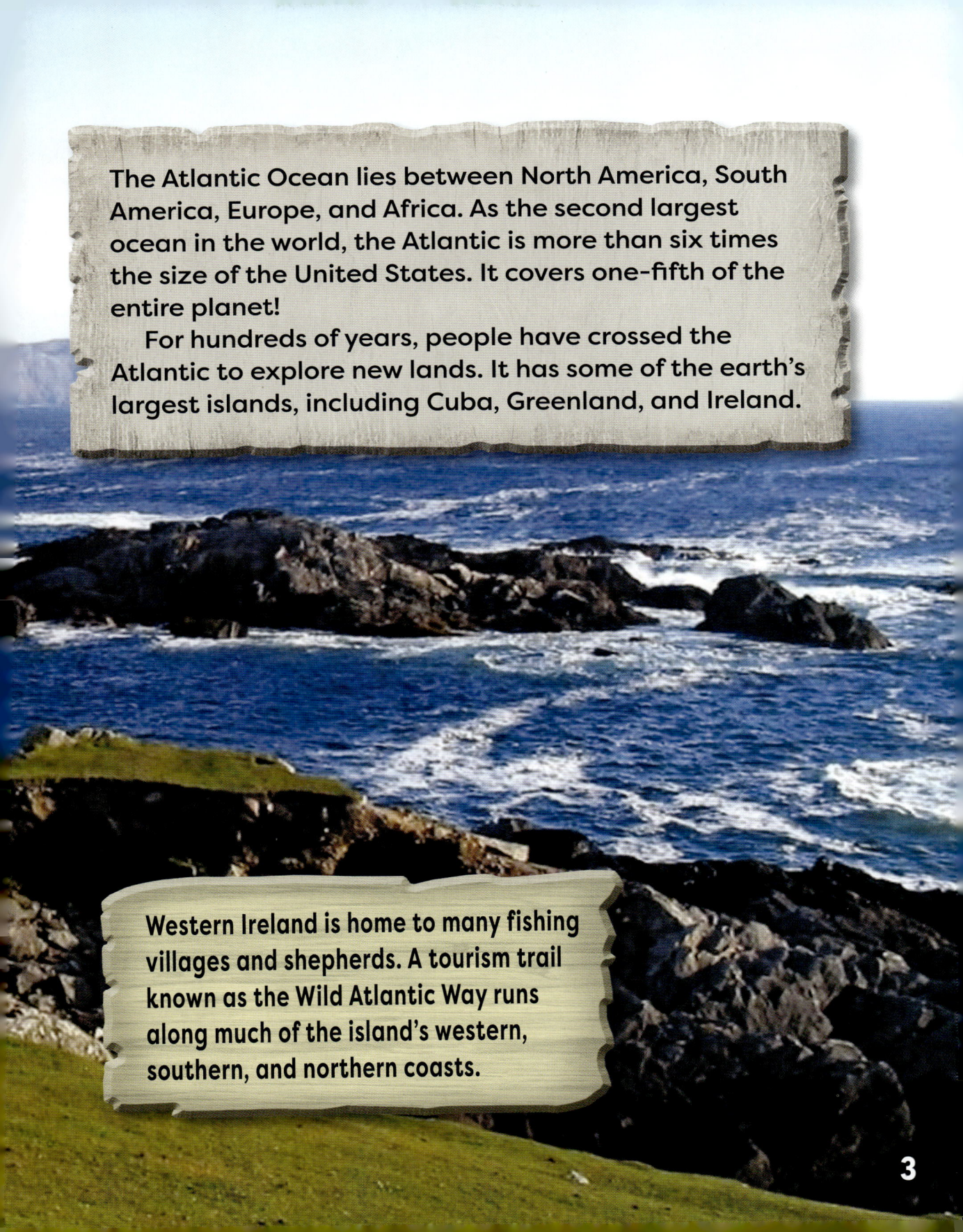

The Atlantic Ocean lies between North America, South America, Europe, and Africa. As the second largest ocean in the world, the Atlantic is more than six times the size of the United States. It covers one-fifth of the entire planet!

For hundreds of years, people have crossed the Atlantic to explore new lands. It has some of the earth's largest islands, including Cuba, Greenland, and Ireland.

Western Ireland is home to many fishing villages and shepherds. A tourism trail known as the Wild Atlantic Way runs along much of the island's western, southern, and northern coasts.

The Atlantic cod can travel 200 miles (321.9 kilometers) to reach breeding grounds. They swim the ocean hunting other fish and crustaceans.

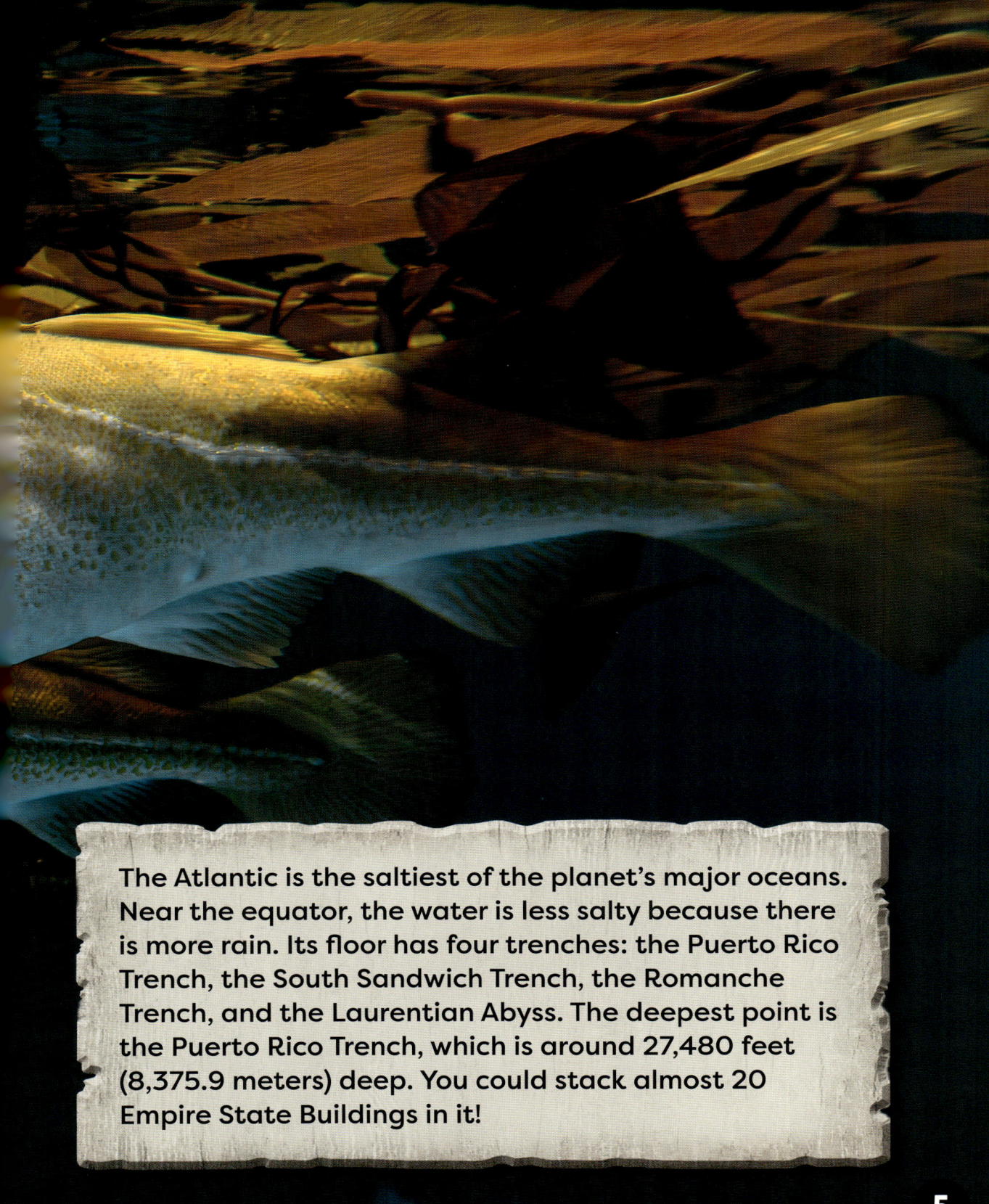

The Atlantic is the saltiest of the planet's major oceans. Near the equator, the water is less salty because there is more rain. Its floor has four trenches: the Puerto Rico Trench, the South Sandwich Trench, the Romanche Trench, and the Laurentian Abyss. The deepest point is the Puerto Rico Trench, which is around 27,480 feet (8,375.9 meters) deep. You could stack almost 20 Empire State Buildings in it!

The Atlantic Ocean has more than 50 types of seagrasses. They grow fast and some grow as tall as 200 feet (61 meters).

Many creatures eat the seagrass, from larger creatures like green sea turtles and manatees to tiny creatures like seahorses. Seahorses even grasp onto the seagrass with their flexible tails, so they can stay hidden and keep themselves from drifting in the ocean while they sleep.

Besides being a food source, seagrass is also a perfect hiding place for horseshoe crabs, especially when they are young. The horseshoe crab has long pointed tail called a "telson," which it uses to flip itself over if it gets stuck upside down!

The Mid-Atlantic Ridge is the planet's largest mountain range. It reaches from Iceland all the way to Antarctica (ant-AHRK-ti-kuh) and is home to some of the ocean's most unusual species. In Thingvellir National Park in Iceland, you can see some of the Mid-Atlantic Ridge that rises above the water. You can even snorkel or scuba dive around the the mountains and rifts in the park's lake.

The worm-like creature shown here next to a remote-controlled diving robot exploring the Mid-Atlantic Ridge is actually made of many tiny creatures. It is known as a "siphonophore." Most siphonophores are bioluminescent, meaning they glow.

The Atlantic octopus has several tricks to keep it safe. It can change colors instantly to match its surroundings. It can shoot ink to confuse predators. If it has to, it can even leave one of its arms behind to escape!

The common octopus will eat almost anything it can catch, and it has a beak it can use to break into mollusk shells. You might think of an octopus as having eight tentacles **(TEN-tuh-kuls)**, but really it has eight arms! Tentacles only have suckers on the end, while octopus arms have suckers on the whole length.

The green sea turtle is the largest hard-shelled sea turtle, growing up to 5 feet (1.5 meters) long. They are known as "green" sea turtles because they have a layer of green fat beneath their shell. This fat is green because they only eat seagrass as adults. They are the only adult sea turtles that eat almost no meat.

Sea turtles travel long distances to return to special nesting beaches where they climb out of the ocean and lay their eggs. The babies crawl to the water as soon as they hatch. They can live up to 100 years!

Sharks abound in the Atlantic Ocean. The great white shark is probably the best known. Great white sharks have an amazing sense of smell. If just a single drop of blood is floating in 10 billion drops of water, the great white shark can smell it! The great white shark also has hundreds of sharp, jagged teeth it uses to grab seals and sea lions. It can hear them from miles away.

The whale shark is the largest shark in the Atlantic Ocean. It is 40 feet (12.2 meters) long—that's as long as a school bus! The great white shark is only half that size.

The mako (MAY-koh) shark swims faster than any other shark in the world.

16

Even though pygmy sharks are small, they will follow their prey over 6,000 feet (1,828.8 meters) down into the deep water. They return to the surface water every night.

The shortfin mako shark has a bright blue or purple top fin. These sharks swim very fast, reaching almost 50 miles (80.5 kilometers) per hour for short times. This is almost as fast as cars go on the highway. The pygmy shark is one of the smallest sharks in the world, measuring only around 9 to 10 inches (22.9 to 25.4 centimeters) long. It snacks on crabs and squid in the colder parts of the Atlantic.

ROVs carry lights and powerful cameras. They can skim along the ocean floor, where it is too dangerous for divers to go.

The smallest known type of dumbo octopus is only as big as a spoon.

The creatures living deep in the Atlantic Ocean can survive where it is very dark and cold. Scientists use remotely operated vehicles (ree-MOHT-lee OP-er-ay-ted VEE-hih-kuls), or ROVs, to film species that live over 20,000 feet (6,096 meters) deep, including types of dumbo octopuses. Dumbo octopuses live deeper in the ocean than any other octopuses. Their name comes from the elephant ear–like fins they have above their eyes.

Some of the species found in the deepest parts of the Atlantic Ocean include types of jellyfish, plankton, corals, and basket stars. Basket stars are a type of animal called a "brittle star," and they are cousins to the sea star. Each star has a huge web of branching arms that it uses to catch drifting plankton for food. Basket stars don't have any blood, and they live up to 35 years.

The purple deep-sea acorn worm was first discovered deep in the Atlantic Ocean. Most acorn worms usually live in the sediment on the seabed. They eat sand, mud, and other organic materials.

Harbor seals are also known as "common seals" because there are so many of them in seas and oceans around the world. They can be brown, silver, tan, or gray and each seal has a unique spot pattern. They can grow to over 6 feet (1.8 meters) long and weigh up to 370 pounds (167.8 kilograms).

Baby harbor seals, called "pups," are born on the shore. They can swim within hours and grow quickly because their mothers produce fatty milk. They can double in size in less than a month.

The giant manta ray is the largest ray in the world. They can grow up to 30 feet (9.1 meters) long. That's almost as long as a telephone pole! They swim along in the ocean currents and must always stay in motion so water moves over their gills. Sometimes they eat by filtering plankton out of the water. Their front fins help to move the water and food into their mouths.

Giant manta rays are very smart and have great vision. They have the largest brain of any fish, and it's been proven that they can even recognize themselves in a mirror.

Baby king penguins are covered in dark brown fuzzy down feathers, which they will lose later. They spend their first 40 days with their parents, who take turns protecting them and searching for food.

King penguins are the second largest type of penguins in the world. They live in the southern Atlantic Ocean mostly on islands or parts of Argentina. Adult king penguins are very colorful. They have yellow-orange feathers on their chest, orange patches on their cheeks, and orange on their lower beak.

Atlantic puffins are also known as "sea parrots" because of their colorful beaks. They lose the colorful outer layer of their beak during winter, when they fly out to sea. They don't return to the land until the spring. Then, they live on coastal cliffs and islands, ride the ocean's waves, and dive and swim when searching for plankton, fish, or crabs to snack on.

In the spring, when puffins return to land, pairs dig burrows and building nests inside. They usually lay one egg per year. Baby puffins, known as "pufflings," have black fluffy down feathers.

FURTHER READING

Books

Burleigh, Robert. *Night Flight: Amelia Earhart Crosses the Atlantic*. New York: Simon and Schuster, 2011.

Gonzales, Doreen. *The Mighty Atlantic Ocean*. Berkeley Heights, NJ: Enslow Publishers, 2013.

McClellan, Ray. *The Bermuda Triangle*. Minneapolis, MN: Bellwether Media: 2014.

Rudolph, Aaron. *The Unsolved Mystery of the Bermuda Triangle*. Mankato, MN: Capstone, 2016.

Spilsbury, Louise, and Richard Spilsbury. *Atlantic Ocean*. Portsmouth, NH: Heinemann, 2015.

Web Sites

Britannica: "Atlantic Ocean"
https://www.britannica.com/place/Atlantic-Ocean

Science Kids: "Fun Ocean Facts"
https://www.sciencekids.co.nz/sciencefacts/earth/oceans.html

GLOSSARY

plankton (PLANK-tin)—Tiny plants and animals that float in the ocean.

predator (PREH-dih-ter)—An animal that hunts other animals for food.

remotely operated vehicle (ree-MOHT-lee OP-er-ay-ted VEE-hih-kul)—A moving robot that is controlled from far away.

tentacle (TEN-tuh-kul)—A long flexible organ used for holding, feeling, or grasping.

trench (TRENTCH)—A long, narrow gash in the ocean floor.

PHOTO CREDITS

INDEX

Awesome Creatures of the Atlantic Ocean is a revision of *Water Planet: Life in the Atlantic Ocean*, originally published in 2018 by Purple Toad Publishing, Inc. Reproduction of its contents is strictly prohibited without written permission from the rights holder.

Paperback ISBN 979-8-89094-176-3
Hardcover ISBN 979-8-89094-177-0

Library of Congress Control Number: 2024949953

To learn more about the other great books from Fox Chapel Publishing, or to find a retailer near you, call toll-free at 800-457-9112 or visit us at *www.FoxChapelPublishing.com*.
You can also send mail to:
Fox Chapel Publishing
903 Square Street
Mount Joy, PA 17552

We are always looking for talented authors. To submit an idea, please send a brief inquiry to acquisitions@foxchapelpublishing.com.

Fox Chapel Publishing makes every effort to use environmentally friendly paper for printing.

Printed in China